GW00455190

Table of Contents

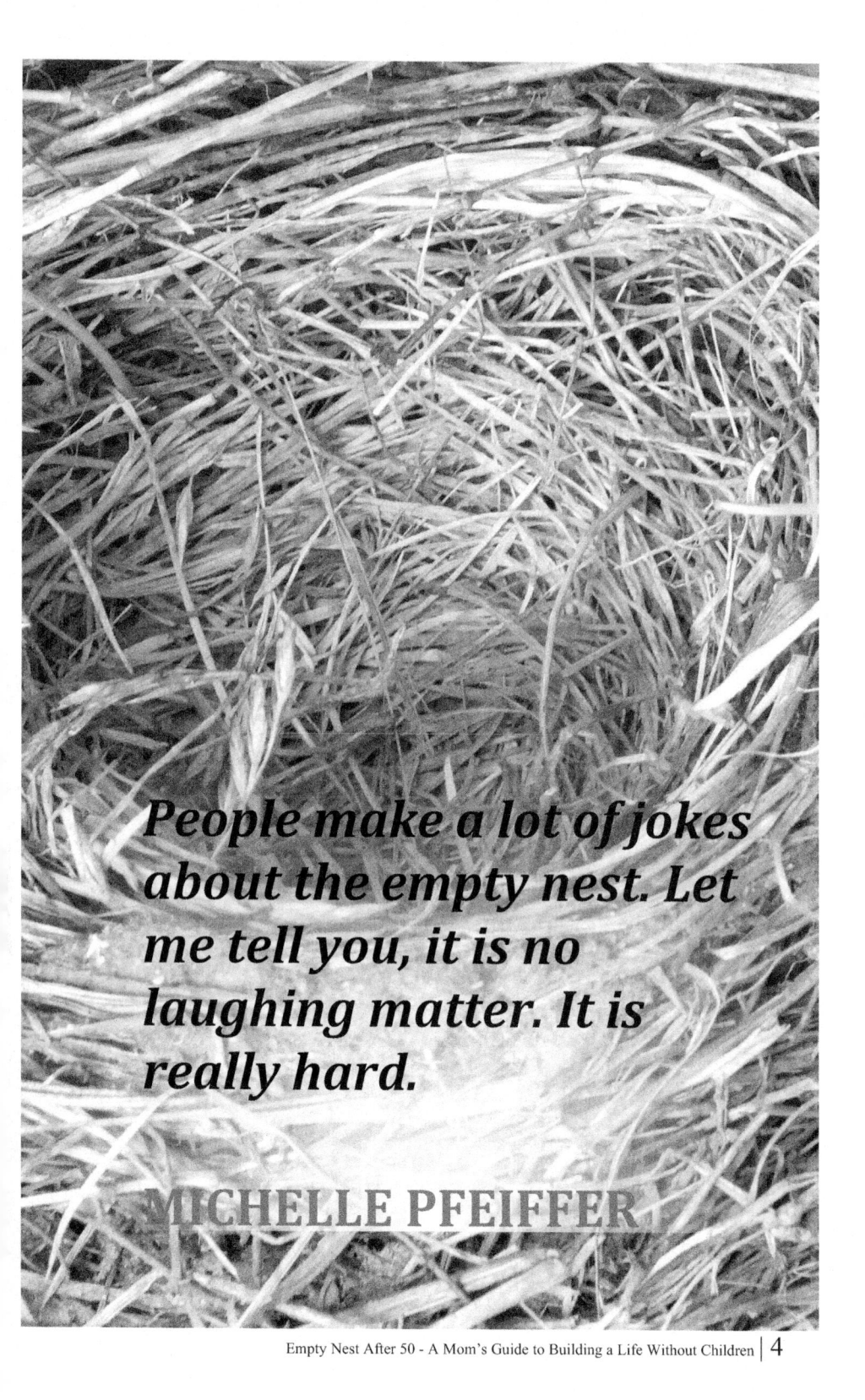

People make a lot of jokes about the empty nest. Let me tell you, it is no laughing matter. It is really hard.

MICHELLE PFEIFFER

Introduction

No child stays home forever, hopefully. The day you had your first child, it was inevitable that this day would come. You were destined to be an empty-nester-mom the day your first child came into the world. You are rendered empty nest by college, jobs, or marriage. Either way, they are going to grow up and grow out.

You may have spent pretty much your entire adult life so far raising your kids. If you're over 50, you may even be fostering the notion that your life is nearly over. You suddenly feel a double whammy of empty-nest plus mid-life crises - all at the same time.

So, what now?

What are you going to do? The main focus of your life is gone. The primary buffer in your marriage is gone. You're likely to have greatly reduced contact with all the other moms once your children no longer share classes, sport activities, birthday celebrations, and other high school activities.

You're likely to have more money, time, and freedom than you have had in a very long time, but what are you going to do with them?

How are you going to deal with the fact that for an extend length of time, you're not going to see or speak to your child each day?

How will you manage your relationship with your spouse? Kids are a lot to have in common, and that commonality is greatly reduced now that they are gone. What does the future hold for you and your significant other?

Fortunately, there are many things you can do to transform that void in your life and build an exciting, more intimate, and fulfilling future!

In this book, we will discuss the following topics as we explore strategies for dealing with Empty Nest Syndrome and how to build a life as a mom over-50 without children:

Chapter 1: The Signs, Symptoms, and Challenges of Empty Nest Syndrome: Youwill discover how living in an empty nest can affect your life and emotional outlook. You will also discover the many challenges that managing an empty nest can pose.

Chapter 2: Marriage: Children are a challenge and an advantage in a relationship. When the last child leaves the nest, it's just you and your spouse. Is that going to benefit your relationship or make it more challenging?

Chapter 3: Staying in Touch: Just because your child is leaving home, doesn't mean you can't stay in touch. However, it likely means you won't be able to stay in touch every single day Especially if you have boys. Learn how to find a communication schedule that works for everyone involved and get used to the power of and importance of social media.

Chapter 4: Hobbies: You have free time now, so it's time to find a hobby or two to fill the time. It's time to have fun while doing this.

Chapter 5: Travel: You can finally visit those places you have always dreamed of seeing. Now that all kids are out of the home, no kids mean fewer plane tickets and hotel rooms, hence money free money to spend.

Chapter 6: Social: Humans are social animals, everyone needs a social life of some sort. Create the social life you desire and fill some of the void left by your children leaving. Who says an empty nest can't be fun? Life is what you make it.

Chapter 7: Life Over 50 and After Children: In this chapter, you will figure out what you want from your life and how to get it. The basic process you will learn in this chapter can be used to accomplish nearly any goal.

Let's get started!

We were empty nesters, our last-born child having departed for Duke. Meredith decided we needed a dog to fill the vacuum. She heard about a litter in Colorado sired by Chopper, the legendary avalanche dog at the top of Aspen Mountain.

TOM BROKAW

Chapter 1: The Signs, Symptoms, and Challenges

Empty Nest Syndrome is the grief many parents feel when their children move out of the family home. This syndrome is more common with women especially the ones that played the role of primary care taker of the child that moved out.

Empty nest syndrome can become a type of psychological disruption if not well managed. As such, there are signs and symptoms that commonly occur in those suffering from this affliction. And like any other disease or disorder, there are challenges associated with Empty Nest Syndrome.

Empty Nest Syndrome might not be a recognized clinical disorder, but the effects of the pain and sadness of letting go are real. Some of those effects are:

Your marriage may become more challenging.
While children can be a real challenge for a marriage,
they can also keep a shaky marriage together. A not
so spectacular marriage can look relatively healthy
while the children are still young and present, but
that stability quickly crumbles when the last child
has left the home.

Children provide a distraction. You and your
husband have been able to put your attention on
your children instead of on each other. High school
kids have a lot going on: class, friends, dates, dances,
parties, sports, band, college visits and applications,
and other after school activities can be a perfect
distraction for a not so strong marriage.

Children provide a buffer. Most parents are
reluctant to argue and fight in front of their children.
Your kids can help to keep the peace, even if it's
unknowingly.

Children provide a shared purpose. You and your husband place a high priority on the children and ignore your relationship. Taking care of the children are shared goal and ideal. When the youngest leaves the house, that shared purpose would have largely evaporated.

There is a change in the dynamic of the home, even among the best of marriages when the children leave the home. Regardless of the quality of your marriage, expect to face some challenges in recalibrating your relationship when you are finally alone.

Your friends may not be understanding. Many parents dream of the day the children finally leave the house, and their bedroom can be turned into a reading room, giant closet, or an extra guest room. Many parents will fail to understand your pain when you are not thinking along that line. Hence, you might not receive the kind of sympathy you were hoping for from friends with younger rowdy kids. Your circle of friends might shrink as a result.

Depression is a significant health threat.
Depression is real and not a joking matter regardless of the cause. It can become a real issue when the children are gone from your home.

Loss of sense of purpose. Children for most women, provide a sense of purpose in their life. Most mothers live and breathe their children. Mothers have responsibilities and duties to perform in order to ensure their children are receiving everything they need. All of this responsibility and purpose evaporates practically overnight when the kids leave home for college, a job, or simply decide to move out.

Loss of identity as a parent. When asked the question "tell me about yourself", most mothers start with "I am a mother of ...... children" sometimes before telling them your name. We all identify ourselves with certain groups, whether they be a gender, profession, religion, body type, ethnicity, and so on, but the identity of being a mother is the most defining identity for many women and so many women lose themselves in the routine of motherhood. Hence, the pain and confusion associated with losing that identity is considerable.

Anxiety/stress over your child's welfare. Parents always worry about their kids, but at least you have a better chance of identifying challenges and helping when your child is still living at home. It's natural to worry and wonder how your child is doing. It can be extremely frustrating and scary to be out of the loop. I have a 33-year-old son who I still ask what he ate for breakfast or dinner because I care and worry that he is not feeding well.

Feeling of rejection: When children leave home, most rarely call their parents, especially boys. This leads to a sense of rejection. This can strain the relationship if not well managed.

Guilt. When your child is still at home, there's still time to make amends, reconcile the hurt, and make up for past mistakes. There's still time to finally take that family trip to Disneyland. You can still create new experiences and pleasant memories of their childhood for your children.

Once a child leaves the home, their childhood becomes final. There's nothing that can be done to change the experience that they had living in your home. Feelings of guilt are common for mothers when the kids leave as they wonder if they did enough or the right thing. But be rest assured that you did your best and release the rest to a higher power.

Self-Medication. What do people do when they feel bad? They find a way to make themselves feel better. Many of the following options people turn to can be unhealthy:

- Overeating

- Drugs or alcohol
- Overspending or shopping
- Spending too much time watching TV or surfing the internet
- Making poor relationship choices.

The urge to change your life drastically. This doesn't have to be a bad thing! You might want to change careers, move to a new location, downsize your home, give yourself a totally new look, or take up new hobbies. There's nothing wrong with any of this provided you're making healthy and intelligent choices.

The challenge is the ability to make the right decision in the midst of the pain, loneliness, stress, anxiety, and hopelessness experienced when empty nested. But with the knowledge and understanding of Empty Nest Syndrome, mothers will be able to identify and reduce the pressure of the negative effect of empty nest after 50.

Empty Nest Syndrome has real symptoms to deal with and challenges to face. See if you can identify these symptoms in yourself and prepare for the challenges that may lie ahead. Planning ahead can save you grief and keep you on track to building a new life that satisfies you.

The biggest change for me as a mom was realizing I needed to put someone else before me. Now the hardest part about the empty nest is learning to put myself first.

- KIM ALEXIS

Chapter 2: Marriage

Marriage by itself is complex and difficult under normal circumstances and after your last child has left the nest can be especially challenging. On the other hand, you also have the opportunity to grow closer than you have been in a long time now that the children a gone from home.

Let's take a look at this scenario and see how you can transform your relationship!

Marriage always has the potential to be challenging, but this new stage in life can be especially difficult. Much of your life has revolved around your kids, their school, sports, academic growth, health, and general care. Your children provided a perfect distraction and a buffer for some disfunction or issues in your marriage. All of which becomes apparent when the children are gone and out of the house.

Now that you and your spouse are left with each other and with fewer distractions to hide any weaknesses in your marriage, it is time to focus on each other, mend the broken pieces, and rekindle your love for each other. The husband at this point has to be sensitive but the wife and mother has a lot to do in reinventing and putting new spark back in the marriage.

Children are a huge and nice thing to have in common. Now, it will be necessary to find new ways to reconnect with your spouse without any readymade distraction. Remember as a mother, your first and only child left is your husband, so it is important to refocus on each other.

Otherwise, it's likely that any hidden marital challenges will bubble to the surface. Keep in mind that research shows that 1 in 4 divorces involve couples over the age of 50!

Strategies for turning empty nest into a blessing for your relationship:

Have a chat. Ideally, you should have a chat with your spouse prior to the children leaving the home. Discuss what you both want for the future. Discover the apprehensions you both have about the future. Think about what you want your life to look like going forward. Discuss your fears and anxiety with each other to reduce the stress.

You might be excited about finally having the house all to yourselves and even have exciting renovation plans. It is very important to have this discussion.

You might even decide to finally downsize your home to reduce financial stress. Move into a smaller home, to a condo, or the location of your choice like on a farm or downtown now that you have not concerns about school districts to worry about.

There's also a grieving process that you can both share and help each other through. Sometimes you think it is only the mother that goes through Empty Nest Syndrome, but this is not completely true. Men go through it too, especially those men that are very involved in the lives of their children, but they want to hide their feelings and "be a man". This is when it is good to have those discussions to pull each other through those stressful times.

Make plans together and separately. It is important to create a shared future for you both. However, you must also create separate plans for the road ahead because you both have differing feelings. A positive, healthy relationship involves some separate activities, instead of your lives revolving around each other. You can plan around each parents' needs and share experiences to avoid the feeling of been smothered. Allow each other separate, alone periods and activities while they heal from the empty nest syndrome

You are two people that have differing interests and goals. Plus, now that you're a bit more mature, your interests may have changed from what they were in the past. Perhaps you'd like to go back to school, and your spouse would like to take up woodworking, a new hobby my help reduce the stress of empty nest.

Creating a common vision for the future with enough flexibility to pursue your own interests as individual is important.

Find common interests and spend time doing them. You can't just sit around holding hands with your spouse every free moment. Explore common interests, pursue it and have fun spending time doing it.

A great way to rediscover your marriage is to share time together doing something enjoyable.

Spend time together with others. Be social. It is necessary to have individual activities, shared activities, and activities you do with other couples or groups of people to avoid boredom.

Go out to dinner, attend church events, volunteer together, or join a softball team. Do something at least once a week that involves spending time with other folks.

Plan a getaway. Once your youngest child leaves the house, have something to look forward to. Move them out and then take a trip! It can be a great way to kick off your new lives together. You can even have this planned out before you are empty nested.

Find some place you have always wanted to go and make the arrangements to travel there.

Get help. Empty Nest Syndrome is a psychological condition, though not a clinical illness. It is a feeling of sadness, grief, anxiety, and loneliness endured by parents and caregivers after their children leave there home to take care and responsibility for themselves. Maybe you need some professional assistance for help with your health and marriage. Sometimes, an outside opinion can point out a few things you're not able to see as a couple. Don't be ashamed to seek therapy.

Many couples eventually split up after the children are no longer part of their daily lives. However, it's not a forgone conclusion. Many marriages survive and even thrive during the empty nest years. It depends on individual efforts and commitment to the marriage.

Prepare as well as you can and adapt to each other. This might be the best thing that could happen for your marriage!

Chapter 3: Staying in Touch

One of the pains women and parents with empty nest syndrome feel is lack of constant companionship and the inability to let go or be completely cut off from their children's daily lives. It's never been easier to stay in contact with others. Social media, video chats, texting, the opportunities are endless and mind-blowing. The avenues of communication are ever readily available. There's no reason you can't stay in regular contact with your children.

However, it takes two to tango. While you might have visions of sharing a video chat with your child each evening, they might have other ideas entirely. Don't be disappointed, be consistent and continue to stay in touch with them.

Consider these ideas for staying in touch

1.   **Get input from your child.** Rather than dictate to your child how and when you're going to communicate, get their input. Discover your child's preferences and then build a communication plan from that information.

●   Decide on a frequency. Your child might not want to hear from mom each day, or each week for that matter. How often will you communicate? What is a frequency of contact you can both live with?

- Tread carefully with social media. Your so daughter doesn't want mom commenting on every single post or tweet.

2. **Send surprise gifts.** Everyone likes an unexpected package. You can send cookies, money, a video game, a sweatshirt, toiletries, or anything else you think your child would like. This is a good time to let your motherly instincts guide you. What would your child love to receive? What does your child need?

3. **Check yourself.** Your child is an adult now, so adjust your conversation tone accordingly. You're not the boss anymore.

4. **Keep it positive.** Make the conversations as enjoyable and upbeat as possible. Tell your child about the good things happening in your life. Skip the negative stuff as much as possible. Ask your child about their favorite class, professor, cafeteria meal, or social activity.

5. **Plan visits. Schedule times to visit your child.** Avoid the pop-in at all costs! Make plans to do

something during your visit. Your child doesn't want to sit in their dorm room with mom.

- For example, go out to dinner, see a movie, take your child shopping, or go for a bike ride. What do you both like to do?

6. **Keep holidays and summer break interesting.** College students don't do well with boredom. Keep things interesting at home. Do things over school breaks. Plan a vacation. Your college student would probably rather lie around in their apartment and watch TV than lie around in your home and watch TV.

Make plans to see your children as often as they're willing to see you. Ensure that your child doesn't feel like you have forgotten about them, but give them room to breathe, too. It is definitely a thin line.

Chapter 4: Developing Hobbies

You may have forgotten over the years, but there have been a lot of things you always wanted to do, but either lacked the time, money, or freedom to pursue them.

Hobbies are a great addition to your life and can provide a lot of wonderful social opportunities, too.

You finally have the opportunity to:

- Write a book
- Join a literary / Poetry group
- Learn the piano
- Learn how to play golf
- Plant a garden
- Learn how to cook like a pro
- Take up running
- Volunteer
- Or anything else you'd like to do

You can start taking advantage of your new freedom!

Consider some of these ideas:

1. Take a look at what you already like to do.

- What are the things you love to do, but haven't been able to do as much as you like? What are the things that can make you forget to eat? What are the things that make time pass quickly?

- Maybe you love to listen to jazz music. You could listen to it more at home. You could go to a jazz club once a week. Or, you could learn to play a jazz-related instrument.

- Do you love to crochet? Maybe you could start a little business on the side.

   - Do you love to garden? Maybe you now have time to enter rose competitions. Or, you could plant your first full-scale vegetable garden.

2. Think back on your past:

- What did you always want to do or try, but never seemed to get around to it? Did you always want to learn how to roller skate? Bake pastries? Train your dog to do tricks?

- What have you enjoyed doing in the past but no longer do because you have kids? Ballroom dancing? Hiking?

- What interests did you have as a child? What activities did you enjoy?

3. Try something interesting and see if you want to continue. Try not to take the search for a hobby too seriously. If something interests you, give it a shot. No one says you have to stick with it for years.

- Take one cooking class
- Try one dance class
- Borrow a friend's tennis racket for an hour
- Try your hand at painting
    - See what you like and go from there. You might decide to give 10 different things a try and then choose the one you like the most.

4.   Consider getting a friend to join you. Some things are better done with a friend, while others are more enjoyable alone. It's up to you to decide whom, if anyone, you want to include in your hobby.

5.   Decide what you want to get out of it. Are you just looking to have fun? Do you want to experience personal growth? Do you want to do something exciting? Are you looking for a hobby that you can turn into an income? Get in shape? There's an enjoyable hobby for every objective.

Hobbies can be a great way to enhance your social life, enjoy your free time, experience personal growth, push yourself, or get back in shape. You might even find a hobby that you can turn into a 1st or 2nd career.

Your child's life will be filled with fresh experiences. It's good if yours is as well.

DR. MARGARET RUTHERFORD

Chapter 5: Travel

Many empty-nester moms love to travel and are determined to make the most of this time in their lives to add to their life experiences.

You can finally travel to those locations that kids don't like. It's less expensive without the kids in tow, too. Maybe you can finally afford that trip to Europe now that there are fewer plane tickets and hotel rooms to purchase.

Consider these benefits that traveling offers you:

1.   Fulfill a dream. Your kids are gone, and you're feeling down in the dumps. What better way to boost your mood than to plan a trip to your dream destination? This might be something worthy of a splurge.

- Create a bucket list of all the places you have always wanted to visit.

2. Where have you considered retiring? You might love the idea of living in Florida. However, if you have never been there, the mosquitos, heat, humidity, and frequent thunderstorms might be an unpleasant surprise.

- This is a great time to visit those places that are on your list of potential retirement locations. Even if you're still several years away from retiring, it's never too soon to start looking.

3. You can travel in the off-season. It can be so much more enjoyable to travel during the off season. This is not possible when you have kids in school. There are fewer crowds, lower prices, and often better weather.

4. Spend a wonderful time with your children. Just because you can travel without your kids, doesn't mean that you have to. Traveling can bring the whole family together for a memorable experience. Travel can be a great way to stay connected to your children as well.

Many empty nesters love to use their newfound freedom to travel to those places they either couldn't afford or weren't interesting to their children. Traveling can be an excellent way to enjoy your new lifestyle. Where do you want to go?

Jobs fill your pocket but adventures fill your soul.

- JAMIE LYN BEATTY

Chapter 6: Social

Mothers often have a very strong bond with their children. Once the children are gone, it's necessary to create other social bonds or to strengthen existing bonds.

If your socializing activities were centered around your children, this can be a challenging part of your life to rebuild. However, there are plenty of people in the world looking for someone to talk to and to spend time with.

Create new, or strengthen old, social relationships and connect with others:

1. **Make a list of long-lost friends**
   Everyone loses touch with friends over the years. Some of these friends might even live in your town. It's not easy to reach out to people you haven't spoken to in ages, but this might

be the right time to rekindle those old friendships.

2.   **Make a list of friends and family** you don't see as much as you'd like. There's also that group of people that you haven't completely lost touch with, but they are no longer in your life significantly. Turn your empty nest situation into an opportunity to have these people in your life in a more meaningful way.

3.   **Dinner plans.** There is a book titled, "Never Eat Alone". This book is about success in the business world, but the idea rings true for everyone. Meals are a great time to socialize. Ensure that you're eating meals with others at least a couple of times a week.

● You could have standing Thursday night dinner plans with your best friend. Or regular lunch plans with your significant other.

● Consider getting groups of friends together and take turns hosting dinner on a regular basis.

4.   **Pursue new activities.** The chapter on hobbies touched on this topic. There are plenty of activities available that can help to boost your social life. Here's a quick list:

• Join a coed recreational sports team: Bowling, darts, softball, and so on.

• Play cards.

• Travel groups

• Yoga class

• Church

• Volunteer.

• Trivia night at the local bar

5.   **Go on a date.** If you're single, you may have felt uncomfortable with the idea of dating. Or maybe you simply lacked the time or interest. Now that you find yourself spending more time alone, perhaps the idea of dating is appealing again.

The world is full of lonely and/or bored people. It's not difficult to find someone you like that's interested in spending time with you. Reconnect with friends and family members. Find a few activities you like to do that require other people.

Endeavour to create new, strengthen old social relationships, and connect with others. Keep going until you have the social life you desire.

I was learning to map my own course and determine my own destination now that my children were no longer at home. A fire burned within my soul, igniting possibilities I previously only dreamed for myself. I was choosing to feather my empty nest with leather and chrome, not a second-hand lover.

DEBI TOLBERT DUGGAR, RIDING

Chapter 7: Your Life After Children

It is time to make a plan for your empty nest situation. Whether your last child is getting ready to leave for college, moving out with their first real job, getting married, or has already left, the situation will be much easier if you have a vision for the future that you can get excited about. There's no reason to pursue a future that doesn't interest you.

Create a List of Focus Areas

It is important to have a target for your future. You can't luck your way into a great life. You must consciously choose it and then create a path to achieve it. After all of your children have left the house, it is necessary to have a new plan for your life. Otherwise, what are you going to do each day? Frustration will set in.

Focus areas are all of the components of '
you want to have. You can have more than ∪
thing in your life.

Here are a few areas to consider in order to prime
your brain and get the ideas flowing:

- Career
- Marriage
- Financial
- Adventure
- Health and Fitness
- Social Life
- Community and Contribution
- Religious and Spiritual
- Personal Development
- Hobbies

What other areas can you think of?

Write down:

Create a Vision for Each Focus Area

all of the components of your future life that are important to you. You might have all or some of these, or a completely different list all together. It's your life, so you get to choose! However, it's best to limit your initial plan to 3-5 focus areas. Spreading yourself too thin is a recipe for poor progress.

Make that list! You're going to need it:

Parents can only give good advice or put them on the right paths, but the final forming of a person's character lies in their own hands.

ANNE FRANK

We think in pictures, so having a clear picture in your mind of what you want your life to look like is critical to moving pass the pain of empty nest. Create a picture in your mind for each of the focus areas you just identified on the list above. Keep playing around with the visualization until it is as exciting as you can make it. Speak it into existence.

You will know that you have created an effective vision when it fills you with excitement, but still feels possible. If it feels impossible, you will struggle to take action consistently. People with goals that feel impossible either never get off the starting line or sabotage themselves quickly. Visualize the possibility, take steps to make it happen though seemingly impossible, and do not allow fear to keep you bound.

Rise up, put on your creative cap and think about all the possibilities. Close your eyes and ask your mind

to give you a clear picture of your ideal version (
one of your focus areas.

The future can hold a lot if you're willing to dream
and work at it! Remember, life is what you make of it
and when you dream it and build it, they will come.

Create an Exciting Vision of the Future:

To create a vision that excites you, follow the steps
below and answering the questions.

1.   What are you feeling? What is the actual
emotion you're feeling? How would you describe it?
Can you adjust the visualization to increase the
positive feelings you are experiencing?

•   If you are experiencing any negative or
nagging feelings, what is the cause? How can you
change the visualization to eliminate those feelings?

•   Rate the experience on a scale of 1 to 10. If you
are at less than a 10, you still have some work to do.
Keep making modifications until you reached a 10.

2.   What are your thoughts? While you are experiencing your visualization, what are you thinking? What are you saying to yourself?

- What changes can you make to the visualization to have even better, more enjoyable, more positive thoughts?

3.   Who else is there? Is there anyone else in your visualization besides yourself? How do you feel about having that person there? Would the experience be more positive if it were someone else instead? Would you feel better if you were alone?

- Remember, this is your potential future. You can tailor it as you desire to fit your preferences.

4.   What do you see, hear, smell, and feel? Immerse yourself in the experience. Describe your surroundings. What sounds do you hear? What do you smell? What can you physically feel? Is the air cool or warm? If you're standing, describe the pressure you feel on your feet. If you are sitting, describe that feeling.

- The more realistic and detailed you can make the experience, the more effective it will be.

5.   How likely are you to achieve it? On a scale of 1 to 10, how difficult will it be to accomplish? Consider a 10 to be possible, but very challenging. Go with your guts.

•   When you ask yourself how hard this is going to be, pay attention to what your body and brain tell you. Translate those thoughts, feelings, and body sensations into a number.

•   If the number for the level of difficulty is more than a 10, you might have to back off of your vision for now. You can always revisit this part of your life and create a new target after you have made some progress.

Mothers all want their sons to grow up to be president, but they don't want them to become politicians in the process.

JOHN F. KENNEDY

- It needs to be reasonable. You can't imagine yourself being a foot taller or married to Tom Cruise or Tyler Perry and expect this process to deliver the results you want. Stretch yourself but keep it believable, actionable and realistic.

A truly compelling vision is what will pull you forward into the life you desire but it must be realistic. Just because you're over 50 and your kids have left home doesn't mean you can't have an amazing life.

Your life can be even better in many ways because you now have more time and other resources available to you to actualize those dreams.

Avoid simply accepting what you first imagine. Evaluate your options critically. Play around with the details and make it as compelling as you can. The devil is in the details. Spend as much time you need on this activity to get it exactly right before implementation.

eat this process for each focus of your life.

Creating a Goal That Represents Each Vision

To successfully deal with empty nest syndrome, having a clear vision is helpful in several ways. Setting goals:

• Allows you to fine tune what you want. It is a method to acquire feedback about the suitability of what you want.

• Provides a compelling image that can help to keep you focused and motivated.

• Provides a target for your subconscious to pursue. A detailed vision makes what you're trying to accomplish clear.

• Provides a foundation for creating a specific goal. A goal is necessary for monitoring your progress and measuring your success. For example, it is one thing to imagine your amazing new body in the mirror. It is another to know specifically how many pounds you have lost.

Let's create some goals! A vision is of little to no use without a goal to support it!

The Process to Create Effective Goals:

1.   Looking back at all the work you have done; determine the goals you will need to reach those visions of your future. For example, if you have determined that you need to get in better shape and have a clear vision of what that looks like, what are the goals or steps you need to get there?

- For example, perhaps you decide that you want to lose a total of 25 pounds in a healthy manner.

Nothing you do for your children is ever wasted. They seem not to notice us, hovering, averting our eyes, and they seldom offer thanks, but what we do for them is never wasted.

Garrison Keillor

2.   How long do you believe that will take? Be mildly aggressive but reasonable. Let's suppose that you believe you can lose six pounds per month, so you need four months.

- Pull out your calendar and look ahead four months. What is the date? Record that. Bind your goal to a time.

3.   Create a goal statement. Adapt the following format to your goal.

- *"On or before November 12, 2021, I will have done whatever is necessary to weigh 145 lbs. I will do this in ways that support the health of my mind and body."*

- *"On or before October 1, 2021, I will have done whatever is necessary to increase my income by $2,500 per month. This increase in income will require no more than an extra 3 hours of work each week to sustain. I will do this in ways that are ethical and sustainable."*

- *"On or before December 31st, 2021, I will be dating the man of my dreams. He will meet the following criteria:*
- Between 50-60 years old
- Be over 5'7" in height
- Work out at least 3x each week
- Love animals
- Enjoy cultural activities
- Have employment that he enjoys and permits him to support a middle-class lifestyle or better
- Loves to travel internationally
- And so *on...*

4.   Take note of the measurable components of your goal. Let's take a look at the first example above **"On or before November 12, 2021, I will have done whatever is necessary to weigh 145 lbs. I will do this in ways that support the health of my mind and body."**

- The date is something that can be measured. You know what the date is each day.

- Your body weight. This is also something that can be measured.

- Supporting the health of the mind and body is subjective, but it's still possible to make a judgement of whether or not this criterion is being met.

- As you're working toward your goal, you will be measuring your progress against these criteria.

It is important not to specify how you will accomplish your goal. That's far too limiting and sometimes intimidating. You will find that it is far more effective to be very open to how you accomplish your goal than to place a limit on strategies for achieving the goals.

Conclusion

As a good parent must, you changed your life considerably to accommodate your children's interests and needs most of your life.

The good news now is that you can finally create a life that supports your own needs and desires.

The challenging part is that it's not easy to start over. You're attached to your children and the liveliness they bring to your household.

Listen to the desires of your children. Encourage them and then give them the autonomy to make their own decision.

DENIS WAITLEY

Relationships are challenging, and the presence of children can temporarily smooth over relationship difficulties. Children provide a shared experience and priority for you and your spouse, hence the dynamics of your family changes without them.

Once the children are gone, all of those hidden issues tend to surface in a dramatic way. Having children can be stressful for a relationship. Children leaving can be even more stressful for a relationship.

This chapter in your life is a **New Beginning** for a life that is more focused on you.

It is a wonderful opportunity to just be you and do you! Recognize this opportunity and take full advantage of it to make the next chapter exciting and fulfilling.

You will be so glad you did!

Love your children enough to let them go and proper.

Trust them enough to make their own mistakes and own it.

Allow yourself to enjoy this phase of your life instead of living in a stressful panic mode.

Give yourself permission to trust that you have done a good job with raising and readying your children for the world.

Remember Proverbs 22:6 says
"Train up a child in the way he should go, and when he is old, he will not depart from it

Enjoy the Empty Nest and begin to fill it with new memories.

Be happy and relax. You have raised a good and independent child.

NOTES

Printed in Great Britain
by Amazon

84698665R00037